Gallery Books
Editor Peter Fallon

LIVE STREAMING

Conor O'Callaghan

LIVE
STREAMING

Gallery Books

Live Streaming
is first published
simultaneously in paperback
and in a clothbound edition
on 19 October 2017.

The Gallery Press

Loughcrew
Oldcastle
County Meath
Ireland

www.gallerypress.com

ISBN 978 1 91133 723 2 *paperback*
       978 1 91133 724 9 *clothbound*

A CIP catalogue record for this book
is available from the British Library.

Live Streaming receives financial assistance
from the Arts Council.

Contents

Acknowledgements are due to the editors of the following publications where some of these poems, or versions of them, were published first: *Antiphon*, *Poetry* and *The Poetry Review*.

for my four brothers

'Hearts of one purpose . . . '

Grace

They're coming to collect
the table I'm writing on.
They texted a while ago
to say they were leaving
a suburb four miles south.
Midweek, early evening:
traffic should be light.
I thought of sitting here
in gratitude, once more,
as long as supper lasts.
VINTAGE JOB LOT. My ad
hung weeks unanswered
in the whole foods co-op.
Then yesterday they called
to ask if I'd sell piecemeal.
Happily. The sun has drifted
slantwise of our building.
In the back lane behind me
two kitchen porters smoke
in what could be Cantonese.
For six years my things have
waited for the party I was
always threatening to throw.
There's the door . . .

               They've been
and gone and bought the lot!
They were tremendously sweet:
she, Flemish, full of chat;
a fiancé with beard and bearing
of some prince in waiting.
They came for my table just
and took a shine to everything.
We laughed and lugged it all
to her employer's truck

parked running in the lane,
shook hands, wished luck
and hugged, for heaven's sake.
I came indoors to find
this notebook open on the floor
beneath my broken bread.
Thank you sideboard fetched
halfway across the Fens.
Thank you captain's chest,
handmade plywood bed,
mess benches from the war.
Thanks to all those friends
I shipped on for a song.
Thank you rooms in shade
that might yet prove to be
night already happening.
Thank you echoes echoing.
I have more hope in me
than I'd have ever guessed.

Trailer Park Études

THE STARS

The nights midweek are secrets kept.
No soul on site, no signal/bars,
and zilch for company except
a zillion bright disarming stars.

I'll flit through ambers, quicker, higher.
I'll break each hamlet's STOP or YIELD.
I'll fix some noodles, start a fire
and climb up to the topmost field.

The stars at first are sparse, unclear.
They surface in that drag between
the darkened grass and stratosphere,
the powder blue and bottle green.

They blossom, thick and fast, in droves.
They pulse, in clusters, magnify.
The smoke that's my potbelly stove's
frays outwards through each needle eye.

I'll head below. I'll char till dawn
some apple logs down to their core.
By pewter light when stars have gone
I'll do a bit, a little more.

THE RAIN

You live inside its sound effects
whole weeks on end: its pin machine,
its cardboard drum, its soft-boiled eggs,
its silent-running submarine.

It's like the god of liquid rub-
ber stirred at dawn to slip downstairs
and sip a cigarette, to drub
his fingertips on solid layers

you poured across last summer's drought.
You love it, learn to, as it slows,
and even as you come to doubt
its dribs and drabs and pigeon toes.

Forget the welcome rain outstayed.
For days the leaves are parchment sheet
and wind hangs chimeless in the shade.
Still rain remains the point of heat.

The rain is near. Like everything,
it's best those seconds just before:
the broadleaf's backwards canvas sling,
the fly strip flapping through the door.

THE WIND

The wind's this ancient bloke below
who chunters 'we', who wheezes 'us',
though no one else will come or go.
You want to ask the wind 'Who's *us*?'

but hold your tongue till, in your head,
the wind and him have somehow mixed,
the type of wind that loves a shed
and banging on of things not fixed:

a belt-and-braces year-round wind,
a kiln-dried cobwebbed hardwood wind,
a greenhouse wind, a treebound wind,
an end-of-season car-boot wind,

a padlocked shower unit wind,
an upturned wheelie dumpster wind,
a channel not quite tuned-in wind,
a hollow flight-path thunder wind,

a dog-eared wind, a knocked sign wind,
a spouseless phantom ocean-blown
autumnal graveyard Scots pine wind
who speaks in plurals, moves alone.

THE GRASS

One night last June, in cups, in love
with pickled gin from bubbly flutes,
our clothes in coils about the stove,
we climbed the dark in birthday suits.

It's true! The grass was mown that day.
Like hippies chained in meadow flowers
we tripped above the cut and lay
in blades of petrol suede for hours.

We listened to the lowing black.
We giggled, kissed. We possumed dead.
We woke as flesh and straggled back
like beasts to parlour, dressed, then read.

We trafficked grass in bedspreads, shoes,
and never spoke of that again
through winter's interregnum blues,
of being spooked by skin, of when

the only care we had was grass,
the only stir for miles around
our freezing bones, our clinking glass,
our dying to be rumbled, found.

Live Streaming

Old thing,
to what do
we owe this
most recent

inkling? An indoors
offshore gust?
Or air displaced
by a practice

swing in gloaming?
I know this
much: it comes
to us, to life,

that is. I get
now how the still
point comes
to life and we've

but to wait.
Late father,
better than never,
come to life.

Two Thousand and Nine

The purchase of a triplex repo goes through.
The postgrads upstairs worship *Remain in Light*.
My father has four years still to squander.
'And the beat goes on, and the beat goes on . . . '

There's a mattress on cement painted cream.
There's comfort in the chants and footfalls
of away fans from Bavaria, the Basque,
like horses wild in the lane beside my head.

At any one time I've a rice kilo, a cider flagon.
I've stopped hearing the extractor vents
of the dim sum buffets and teppanyaki grills.
My son and daughter wish to be told the truth.

Easter is deafening. Our early bird is black.
There's another person, whose magic number
their old man is. I must wait to be contacted.
They leave. For months we're hardly speaking.

My proximity to my father is not invisible to me.
Bank or flight crashes? I win driftwood online,
wend across the Fens and lose all bearings home.
'And the beat goes on, and the beat goes on . . . '

Like one interrupted repeatedly midstream
I say 'Where was I?' to reduced-to-clear shelves,
parking spaces, the letterboxes' pigeon traps,
the map of a campus farce on my big wall.

Such exiles as one becomes an epicurean of,
industrial backwaters as one seems drawn to,
hurt no less for having no one else to blame!
My mezzanine rings. Too out on a limb not to,

I have phone sex with a pantry in Lincoln,
a limo in Virginia, a cubicle in Brighton.
Death threats and pity pints are equal friends.
My past life was in town and asking for me.

A Glass of Water

I pour a glass of water for myself.
I watch what greys it gathers from the room.
It's not to drink. I want the wanting of
a glass and water sleep can come between.
The glass of water sits there half the year.
Its level drops. Its bubbles bloom and burst.
I get the glass of water's hardly you,
and still I rise to mouthing arid toasts:
to hunger, thirst; to bliss that goes without;
to love abstained, the lull until the flood;
to near enough to touch it hurts, and not;
all windblown wishes, thistles in a field.
I tilt the glass of water to my lips.
I hold like this, before the wanting stops.

The Swimming Pool

has a bamboo pergola, a film of tarp. It belongs exclusively to the half-brother's portion of the hill. Ulrich. Ulrich is territorial and seldom present. Should Ulrich present himself, the brief says, tease remotely. Make it seem all and sundry have been dipping in his absence. A gecko flickers the brickwork. An ass bellows vespers. Just when it seems something so prosaic could never come to pass, Ulrich's people carrier is in the courtyard, his shutters open and VIETATO L'INGRESSO obstructs his access. Nothing fazes him. Not birdsong mimicked. Not draped towels. Not even the spectre, face it, of his sister's tenant treading the cobbles in flip-flops and little else. The air fills with children yelping. The night is rich with chlorine. Below, a band is playing covers in the grounds of a hotel. Does the singer know what she is singing? Or are the lyrics sounds mouthed to a beat? From the terrace downward there are steps bypassing the campanile, the basins at the washroom's door, the woodshed. They yield to a public track that deadends at a circle of gates. Just before, in the verge, hangs a chain of plastic white-and-red and PRIVATA printed onto a sleeve of acetate. Here the family's land ascends. Through palm frond silhouettes, the plumbed oblongs of a caravan park abandoned around the millennium, a pine copse, the back of Ulrich's block rears into view: its shuttered oranges, its burbling deep indoors, its swimming pool's zanzara-addled gloss. The water feels room temperature, viscous, thick with floats and foam noodles. 'Hallo?' Ulrich is on his terrace. With each head-tilt his slidescreen's opal is mirrored twofold in his frameless varifocals. Something akin to an electronic anti-algae snake times on and thrashes on the floor. Ulrich signs off, approaches. 'Buonasera, please?' He is no longer whispering. A warm lungful and under. Concentrate on light, tiles of it wobbling overhead, bubbles of it slipping out. How befuddled Ulrich looks, peering into opaque black. How quiet it is. How clear things get. Drink light in. It is as good as human. The light is all but flesh and blood.

My Father Hangs Around the House Far More

My father hangs around the house far more now he's dead.
He has even quit the hooch.
No white-knuckle ride this time,
no chaining pots of tea
to knock a hole in some unslakeable thirst.
One day he just stopped.
You have to respect that.

He keeps the place immaculate.
Also, there's no more *plámás* or endless ready-salted yarns.
Now his words happen the way
remote islands happen
to be surrounded by silent sea.
He is, in fact, every inch the guy I've always fantasized being.

Granted, the attic clattering at all hours got a bit much.
He claims he was looking for a ball
sliced onto Laytown Strand
decades before I was born.
I had only to raise it once.
Since that once? Not a peep.

He's been devouring *Anna Karenina* for weeks.
He says the difference of emphasis in the original is really striking.
Maybe I'm missing something.
Last I checked, Russian wasn't one of his languages,
he hadn't read any of the translations
and realism in general was never his speciality.

Still, it brings out a glimmer of his old self.
After every chapter he slaps it shut
and paces the rug with fists balled in his slacks' back pockets
and with that smile and wild faraway look in his eyes
he always had between placing a bet and the race.

'Some girl, that Anna,' he laughs, 'some madam, that Karenina.'
He is clearly oblivious as to how it ends.
No way he's hearing it from me.

Nostalgia

for Tommy

I'm nostalgic for Chorlton-cum-Hardy Golf Club.
I know! Nostalgia's weird like that.
The good stuff you forget.

There was a huge elm behind the last, as from a story.
All the members had mohawks, including OAPs.
Or is that just me and memory being faulty

and fanciful? Possibly. Why did I never play?
I dropped you, saw your oneball off and spun away.
Too plot-lost, fogbound, forty,

I was. What a silly moo! Forgive me.
It's possible too I was spinning out even then
to meet nostalgia circling back inevitably

to this and Chorlton-cum-Hardy of all places,
where a city we lived in frays on pylon, Mersey,
an airport's shimmering acres,

arriving as late as always to fetch among
such miscellaneous shadows my only son,
asked too often to belong.

Knitted Roadkill

My fiancée's ex had this crazy aunt.
The grand-progeny of two first-cousin unions,
her craziness (since blood will out)
saw her knitting roadkill she laid then on the verge.
Badgers mostly: their organs unfurled, their little faces startled.

There is no allegory at play,
nor can we attest to the verisimilitude of her art.
We say this only that its truth be handed down.
'Knitted roadkill,' they'll ask, 'is that a thing?'
It is now.

A Decade of the Rosary for Gerry Cooney

for Gerard Fanning

Is it me, or do we seem marooned
interminably in 1982? . . . *our trespasses as . . .*
We're upright, deskside, commencing final period
with a decade of the rosary that Gerry Cooney —
deliver us from evil — wins a crown tonight.
There will follow a quiz on humanism.
Cicero wrote law. Petrarch worshipped Laura,
from 'afar'. He never laid a glove on her.
Gerry Cooney's left cross drops like logs
felled on Long Island . . . *and blessèd be the fruit . . .*
She was promised to some important count
when he glimpsed her after mass in Avignon.
We offer prayers of forgiveness, love,
that a chap none of us has set eyes on
(who may be our history master's cousin)
thump lumps out of a Larry we've heard less of.
This before a grilling on the origins of atheism.
Any wonder we're flagging off-message?
Erasmus was born in Rotterdam . . . *now and at the hour . . .*
Mr Cooney leaves slack from one bead to the next
to plead: 'Come on, men, make an effort.'
. . . *ever shall be world without . . .* Whither its end?
A fat kid on the shortcut home behind the brewery
who already worships 'afar' and hopes too much?
I already hope too much and hope's opaque:
black folds in Gerry Cooney's emerald silk,
an ocean's lag between tomorrow morning,
the veil that's shading Laura's face from view.

Where Kimonos Go to Die

My words are speaking about me
behind my back.
I'm sure of it.
It spreads,
that gradual inexorable molecule-
by-molecule outward
dilution of pigment.

Only last week, early birds,
we mused about the name of that hockey star
who fell nose-first at face-off,
whose blood entered the ice's fabric.
It never came to us.
By buzzer the whole rink had dyed flamingo.

Where kimonos go to die
all doors are gooseberry and loaded with springs.
Stationery is the new snow,
gathering in drifts no nib's squid sullies.
One tiptoe into
the parchment backdrop mountain range
can symbolize a hundred miles.
Heavens above!

Some belong. Some are honoured guests.
Some of us, a gloved hand raised,
will leave most worms splitting the bill
and turn into wind.

Soft Rock

1

The roofers are hooked on drivetime
flint gritstone claystone chert
up and down the boulevard their shadows
I am scaffolded in for now

2

It gets in bones   honey-coats   leaves porous
amber sandstone siltstone salt
there are times when all the world's asleep
I am groggy on sentiment

3

on cliché's hungover rust-belt sediment
chalk greywacke mudstone marl
the things that are said when lovers touch
I am parked all month on the street

4

Soft rock from scaffold   footsteps overhead
gypsum conglomerate feldspar till
and if the wind is right you can sail away
I am bound to feel what others feel

H I S   L A S T   L E G S

Relics of old decency. Mourning too. Terrible comedown, poor wretch! Kicked about like snuff at a wake. O'Callaghan on his last legs.
— James Joyce

6.236 *His Last Legs* (London, 1839) is the title of a brief and once-popular two-act farce by the American William Bayle Bernard (1807-75). The charlatan hero of the farce is the stage-Irishman, Felix O'Callaghan, who, as the play opens, is 'shabby genteel' and down on his luck. Once a landed gentleman and 'reigning star of Cheltenham', he has for ten years been the 'football of Fortune', a failure at everything he has touched.
— *Ulysses Annotated:* Notes for James Joyce's *Ulysses*, Don Gifford and Robert J Seidman (University of California Press, 1988)

The curtain pulls back. My little son and daughter. There's a man. A man? I turn the shower off, wrap round, step out. Says he's your dad. They are on the edge of the mattress in their pyjamas. Wait there.

Jimmy has his back to our fire. 10 a.m. He is between the port's early house and serving hours up the town.

You're not welcome. I am holding our door open with one hand, my towel in place with the other. You know you're not. I am leaving wet footprints everywhere. Let's go.

His exit is the last I see of him for fifteen years.

∼

O'CALLAGHAN *enters*, R., *in a shabby-genteel suit, dusty from travelling.*

O'CALLAGHAN So, then, my journey's at an end, and yonder's my destination.
DR BANKS Do you know, sir, I think I've had the pleasure of seeing you before. Your name, I believe, is —
O'CALLAGHAN O'Callaghan, sir — Felix O'Callaghan, of Kilmony Abbey — (*aside*) some years ago.

∼

Felix. Pronounced locally as a rhyme for 'playlists'. There must have been a time we addressed him as 'Dad'. For as long as I can remember we called him 'Jimmy the Jar'. That came about when Ian, third eldest, was mimicking a wrestler and needed a stage persona for his opponent comatose on the mat in front of the fire. Jimmy, James, Hamish . . .

The eldest of us is Felix too. He was born within hours of Kennedy's assassination. Our mother remembers nuns on their knees in the maternity ward. Three days later, in Arlington Cemetery, the state funeral included an honour guard from the Irish Army. One of the cadets was a Felix O'Callaghan of Dundalk. Coincidence, pure and meaningless, but I like it.

~

Our father died in June 2013. I saw him in a coma a week before. Before that? I hadn't seen him since that morning in 1998 when I ushered him from the first house we owned.

He lived on The Square, Blackrock, County Louth, the last thirty years of his life, in the house he had grown up in. He lived with his dying mother the first ten years of those, and then alone for twenty more of ever-widening isolation. The Square overlooks marshes called The Loakers. Due east is the coastline of Lancashire where his own father was born.

A week after the funeral I borrowed our mother's car and his house key. I walked room to room taking pics. I even recorded myself describing matter-of-factly his things.

~

I'm in the entrance hall
the beautiful 1940s parquet floor is really dark
can't have been polished for 30 years
three bags of slippers   a jacket
bits and bobs of pyjamas as well
somebody has prepared them to take to the hospital
or piled them to send to the Vincent de Paul
An old-fashioned rotary dial   works
a slightly more up-to-date touchtone   dead
One pair of brown corduroy slacks
a blue sailor's jumper
hanging off the cast-iron coat rails
There's a downstairs loo
with sliding door and cup handles

cork tiles on the floor are peeling up
the suite is a dirty olive green
on the window sill is shaving stuff
a shaving mirror   dry skin cream

∼

Three of us blubbed at his burial. Three of us didn't. One who didn't came over immediately after: What was all that about?

We owe our mother everything. Without her we would have been lost. But you can't show grief for him. If you do, you get St Augustine: Late have I loved thee!

There is nowhere to put grief. I leave it here, for the time being, in whatever form.

∼

He slept on the mat in front of the fire. He slept on the mat in front of the fire in his suit. We spent a decade stepping over his corpse. He slept on the mat in front of the fire and made business calls from his sleep.

Hello? Mr Campbell?

Always Mr Campbell. Always in an accent slurring North.

Mr Campbell? Felix here . . .

Poor Mr Campbell, out there in darkness just over the border, being summoned nightly from our slumbering father's head.

Mr Campbell? Felix O'Callaghan . . . He'd laugh. What about you!

∼

CHARLES You're from Ireland, I perceive.
O'CALLAGHAN Yes, sir.
CHARLES Any business?
O'CALLAGHAN Why, I have taught the Sciences.
CHARLES In what branch?
O'CALLAGHAN Comparative Anatomy. I've illustrated, for the last six years, how a man, like a chameleon, may live upon air.

～

The day's first fix. I witness it. Once.

A carload heading south to Dublin for some juvenile golf tournament. He brakes at the Windsor, a mile from our gate. He has to settle his stomach.

He can't get the tonic in on top of the gin quick enough. The neck of his Canada Dry is clinking the glass's rim.

Dad?

It looks excruciating, how he clenches his eyes and rocks his head back and releases a minute death-gasp when that cocktail of relief and remorse poured in equal measure courses into his bloodstream.

Dad?

He drags one hand tightly down his face, so that his face drains from puce to ash. He calls another. I am not certain he is completely conscious. I am not sure he knows who we are or even that we are present.

～

A mustard-coloured oilcloth on the table
a tray of dusty condiments
extremely dirty but also extremely neat
On the back of the single chair
a mauve cardigan with suede patches at the shoulders
a white shirt not washed in a long long time
A gas cylinder   quilted oven glove
a white rusty pedestal hob
There's the old standing dresser
that's kind of rather lovely actually
hot chocolate   egg cups   willow pattern plates
boxes and boxes of marrowfat peas for some reason
bags of flour   bags of Tayto   golf tees
This is the kitchen

~

The North made sense of him. His father grew up there. His father's father ran a tobacconist's in Newry. The nearer we came to it the pointier his pronunciation got.

The North was roads like silk. The North was cronies with funny handles — PJ Moane, Mac and Hilary Hoey, Victor Ronaldson — who drove Rovers and held their gin with the best of them and shouted risk and debentures. The North was pro-ams and minor celebrities.

You fellas OK? I have to stand Pat Jennings a jar. We'll be out of here in half-an-hour.

The North was the terminal fug of a clubhouse Sunday, an adaptation of James A Michener's *Centennial* on the box, our father away off in company.

~

I can sing all the words of Neil Diamond's hits, thanks to him. His party piece was 'The Pale Moon'. It is only recently that I have discovered the song is called 'The Rose of Tralee'. Every drab Sunday afternoon in August is still filled with his 7" single of Joe Dolan crooning 'Silent Night'.

I ever tell you, kid, I met Joe Dolan in Mullingar?

You did.

His favourite was James Last. I came up behind him once. He was lost in Last's live cover of 'Chirpy Chirpy Cheep Cheep'. He had his back to the fire. He was facing the big window. He was conducting the front lawn as if our front lawn were some pop orchestra in Strasbourg. He was pointing to familiar faces at the various tables in the rockery, and doling out glassy-eyed winks like roses. He was clapping and chuckling and punching one fist to the beat when he saw me.

～

The split-level sitting room
the key was locked
I always loved this room as a kid
and it is in absolutely appalling condition
the walls are all damp and black with it
three armchairs   a coffee table with items:
the cover of the canary yellow golf bag
that Brian and he won in the Father and Son
a little hexagonal glass case with dried flowers in it
a photo framed of my father and his sister Mary
my father's about 2
In this room their father saw to his children one by one
They queued in the hall
Two lovely Chinese lacquered floral candlesticks
a wicker wastepaper basket full of hats and gloves
a floral patterned fireguard   a row of books
Lots of photographs of my cousins

36

hard not to be jealous of my first cousins
There's an electric fire   Christmas shopping bags
a brown tweed fedora   a red radio
I slept in here too   just remembered that
after Grandpa died Grandma couldn't be alone
me and Ian took turns to stay over
pretty sure I slept in here on a daybed

~

I run away from school. I run away to the golf club. A Tuesday morning in winter. The clubhouse is desolate. I pot the pool table's cueball for hours. Mr Fanning comes up in a Panama hat from the secretary's office.

What's the meaning of this?

I am halfway down the road when Jimmy surfaces in our Hillman Hunter. That evening the sitting-room door is shut. I am to go in and explain myself. He is in his suit, staring elsewhere, summoning his inner patriarch. He is taking this personally.

If I've done something now's your chance.

I sing dumb. He rambles in metaphors. Sometimes a tyre gets too much air in it. In the metaphor he is the tyre and drink is air. It is all I can do not to laugh in his face. And there was I almost hoping he might have the balls, finally, to belt me.

~

DR BANKS   I presume, sir, you were once well off?
O'CALLAGHAN   Well off, sir? I had one of the best estates in Ireland. I had as fine a set of tradesmen as a man could be born to. It was utterly impossible to be in asier circumstances; but to show you the doom, sir, that from my

37

boyhood hung over me, one of them chose to die, and another to hang himself, till at last, sir, they left me is in a state of destitution. Yes, sir, they had the cruelty to lave me get my own living, after leading me to think that they'd keep me all my days, and even bury me afterwards.

~

A month in the psychiatric hospital in Ardee and he returns like one from the grave. He can't get near enough the fire. He makes pots upon pots of tea, milk and sugar already added. He slugs as though its scald will finally slake his thirst.

Two years, happy ones, that wagon lasts. At one point during them, as if to push him off it, we do a cruel thing. We fill an empty Jameson bottle with cold weak tea and plant it in the cabinet.

We go to the shop. We come back hours later. He is bolt upright in an armchair, bottle empty on the floor, its cap in his fist.

If I find you lads have been acting the maggot . . .

He is trembling visibly. He is livid with sobriety.

Do you hear me?

~

Sober, his drinking cronies receded, replaced by grey AA eminences with names like Tony and Pearse. Guardian angels. They shepherded him to and from meetings. They chain-smoked at our table. They had been through wringers of their own and survived to tell us, repeatedly, their cautionary tales. They arrived with the same metallic body odour and low-wattage sophistry.

All we have is today, Felix. The rest is just a dream.

You could see how stale and desiccated their decency tasted in his mouth, like gagging on a spoonful of crematorium ash. Even for Jimmy, once barred from The Violet for being too boring, Tony and Pearse were too boring. While they rattled on he receded too: into the hall, out to the gate, back down the road to convivial oblivion.

~

I'm in the living room
a pair of long-handled grass clippers and a gaffe hook
a photo of my grandparents in, I'm guessing, Nice
a pint glass of flowers with filthy water
a pair of aluminium shoe-holders
On the table a Colin Dexter novel
magazines   ketchup   a lot of salt
There's also money I'm going to pocket
for all the Communion money he fleeced off us
On the couch is the aquamarine overnight bag
he had in his hand when I opened the door Tramore 1972
joining us from one of his many dalliances
A naïve seascape of Carlingford Lough
On the ornate teak sideboard
Brian after his hole-in-one in Portstewart
Neil a wee boy with gold hair
lots and lots of boot polish
a stuffed Winnie the Pooh

~

Brian represents Ireland at schoolboy level in Portmarnock. Mam drives us up. Jimmy is nowhere, mercifully back on the razzle.

Mid-afternoon, he lands off his own steam. He is wearing a Tam o' Shanter two sizes too small. He is souped up, whooping a music hall Scottish accent: Och aye, Shooey!

He can be such a hateful baby. Our brother plays for the country and his father — unable to cope with his second son becoming the player he might have been — follows too close behind, audible above dunes and gusts, tailing off every gale of laughter with Basil Brush's Boom! Boom!

~

O'CALLAGHAN Now, then, to use the language of history, I perceive the approach of a domestic convulsion.

~

Your four fingers around our door.

We've been to midnight mass. We've called in to cousins, toasted the season with home-brewed hock. Still 1985, if only just. When Mam turns her key your shadow emerges from the wings.

Sometimes it feels I'm the only one who remembers your four fingers around our door. Inasmuch as memory is: an affray of limbs and shouting, us incrementally squeezing your body back out into the small freezing hours of Christmas morning, the monosyllables of *fuck off you cunt* in one of our voices, and Mam pleading with us not to break the four fingers between frame and door that will be the last part of you to disappear.

~

O'CALLAGHAN So, then, after all my hopes and troubles, I've failed again! Here I am in a strange place, at the close of day, with only one and nine-pence in my pocket . . .

~

I stop writing this. I am under its weather. One whole weekend, I take to the bed. My stepdaughter gives me, for company, a tiny toy budgie which repeats your every word. We christen him Michael. I hold in the button on Michael's throat and say slowly: I am not feeling the Mae West.

I release the button. Michael chirps back: *I'm not falin' the Mae Wesht.*

Do I sound like that? Have my English years rendered me more stagey than I realize? Cliché's ineluctable gravitational pull. To that granular half-light of a bedroom of a Saturday afternoon in January, I say: I miss my father.

Michael chirps: *I miss me feather.*

~

The master bedroom
There is a bed with a very swanky duvet cover on it
Somebody I suspect has put it on
My father never slept in those bedclothes
the lines of the packaging are still visible
There is a cold open fire with cream tiles
a crucifix and holy water on top
an old suction hoover with a pink bag
In the wardrobe a couple of old-fashioned suits
jackets   shirts   a dressing gown
a suitcase full of negatives of old photos
nothing terribly interesting
though that looks like at a guess

the wooden GNR train carriage they lived in across the road
while this house was being built
This is going way back
One small boy in the foreground   possibly Martin
the brother with Downs who died young
The white glare behind must be sea

~

After he was gone we filled his absence with impersonations.
We mimicked his half-cut savouring of 'apparently'. We popped
collars, hooked thumbs in pockets, swaggered shoulders.

I dressed in his clothes. I became his understudy, his stunt
double, his ghost. My party trick was aping his *shit* muttered
at the top of the backswing and following some imaginary
quick-hook left. As if he always knew the thing was lost
before it had happened, but couldn't help himself or stop.

~

His face-saving *scéal* went that he was keeping an eye on his
mother in her dotage. When she died he was keeping an eye
on her house.

For years he still came to cut our hedges. He materialized in
gardening clothes, and slipped away as silently. He looked
embarrassed and defiant. You'd pass him on the drive and
exchange nods. When Mam got home from work we said the
gardener had been.

He stood outside the big window of the sitting room. He
held up an antique golf ball and laughed and shouted: This
Pinnacle belong to any of you lads? When we said zilch he
dropped it in through the small window at the top. It broke
a Wedgwood jug.

~

This is the second bedroom
he obviously used as a dressing room
a whole pile of clothes on the bed
mostly golf cast-offs from my brother
a chest of drawers with an empty wine bottle
and an absolutely ancient Fruitfields jam box
containing loads of news cuttings
that seem to be mostly
— good grief —
reviews of yours truly's books
my anthologies!
I'm laughing
but I'm not sure whether to piss myself or weep
seems to have underlined bits
positive adjectives
several spots in the margin he's written
v good
in rickety red biro
Daddy Daddy   I ask you

∿

I hear his voice speak my name. *Conor.* I wake in the afternoon.

This day just never got light.

∿

O'CALLAGHAN *pulls out a handkerchief and turns away, as though struggling with his feelings.*

∿

He composed additional endings for poems he liked. His favourite was 'Stopping by Woods on a Snowy Evening'. He was convinced the poem was by someone called Dooley. In his version the last stanza of Dooley's famous poem went:

The woods are lovely dark and deep,
but I have promises to keep
and miles to go before I sleep
and miles to go before I sleep.
We all have miles to go before we sleep
or we don't sleep at all.

The allusive, arrogant prick his fourth son had grown into must have felt alien to him. In my company he called all books 'anthologies'. It sounded literary. Between my first publications and those last words we spoke I stumbled on him in gardening scrubs in our mother's kitchen.

I was wondering . . .

The hands cupping his instant coffee shook.

How's your latest anthology coming along?

~

MRS MONTAGUE	At length we're alone, and of course you cannot wonder at my surprise. I really thought that you were dead.
O'CALLAGHAN	Well, I don't say I've been living — I've been a sort of dervish since we parted, a man who wanders and fasts.
MRS MONTAGUE	I heard that you had spent your fortune — that you'd become very dissipated.
O'CALLAGHAN	And can you wonder? what won't a man do to stifle his despair? I won't afflict you with the story of my downfall. Suffice it, that I have passed through every stage of misery, from sunshine and champagne to clouds and heavy wet.

~

Ian met him, up the town. This was long after everything. Long after the turn of the millennium and Jimmy had stopped coming to the house to garden and nobody saw him much at all.

Ian was selling flags outside a supermarket for his son's football team. Jimmy came along. He was rooting coppers from the pocket of his slacks when Ian said: You don't know me, do you?

I know the head alright.

I'm your third son.

Jimmy doubled over with laughter. He spluttered something like: Go on out of that! He hugged his overcoat around himself and swayed off into traffic.

~

The passageway down the right of the house
with a door off from the kitchen
I'm having to remove a couple of baskets
a shopping bag   a bucket   out of the way
I'm having to turn the big key
There is a bolt on it as well
Do I really want to go in here?
The door won't open
I won't force it
If I'm honest I'm also scared
at this late stage I don't want to know
what's behind the door
In my grandparents' day it was always
where the pushmower and coal were kept
It always smelled of mown grass
I'll take a photo of the door locked
That'll do

~

Remember the night he leapt from the bushes?

Who?

Hamish . . . Our darling pater.

I do, she laughs. What has that in your head?

We are on Skype. She is at home. I am in a campus office in Pittsburgh, alone here till summer. Outside is dark. Big snow moving in. We do this most evenings around this hour. We keep one another virtual company. Tonight, for some reason, I am even more inclined than usual to thank her. For minding us. For keeping us all together.

Do you remember his four fingers round the door?

Late have I loved thee!

I keep coming back to his four fingers, I say. It's the nearest I get.

~

There wasn't a day went by I didn't imagine his funeral. Me at the pulpit telling the assembled simpering hypocrites what a drunk and a crook and a thoroughly shit father our father really was.

Now that he is dead there isn't a day goes by I don't imagine myself in his place: a house miles from anywhere, the sea near enough to be audible, a range, a wall of books, a bottle, and all my loved ones lost.

~

RIVERS   Well, sir, I have dispatched a servant; and how is he now?

O'CALLAGHAN   Observe!

RIVERS   Asleep!

O'CALLAGHAN   Yes, sir, as tranquilly as when he rested on his mother's bosom.

RIVERS   I declare, so he is.

O'CALLAGHAN   When he wakes, I've no doubt you'll see a great change in him.

~

I tell a lie. I see him too, during that interregnum. Long after Ian does. Long after we've been to America. Long after there is no 'we' anymore, and I am out on a limb of my own in a foreign city's Chinatown.

I must be home for something. A hand-me-down camel hair overcoat, a head gone fairly white and feathery, walking the opposite direction outside the Ulster Bank.

Any ache the moment has is just that ache of not feeling particularly anything at all. If even that. I don't interrupt him. He is too deep in conversation with himself.

~

Late have I loved Thee! For behold Thou were within me, and I outside; and I sought Thee outside and in my unloveliness fell upon those lovely things that Thou hast made. Thou were with me and I was not with Thee. I was kept from Thee by those things, yet had they not been in Thee, they would not have been at all.

~

47

I am home from school. He is early from the office. Just the two of us. He has a message across the border. He needs a caddy.

The snooker balls in his club are ivory, Victorian, akin to potting rocks. In a supermarket car park in Armagh a wee man lays two flat boxes in our boot and lifts their lids. Is this the mythical Mr Campbell? All the reds, all the colours from yellow to black, are polished resin in nests of tissue.

See yon back road, the wee man says counting his Queen's heads, through Jonesborough and Forkhill? No sense paying import duty.

It is my job watching from the rear seat for unmarked Customs cars. Headlights on dimmers. The drumlins and gloaming of bandit country. What was that? It is my job dispelling whatever shadows he glimpses in his mirror. We're screwed!

There's nothing, I am calling. Keep moving.

The two seem one — my father, his border — the closer he gets us to the line. The nearer safety, the more they come the same. His roads are unapproved. All cars in our slipstream will be unmarked, and phantom.

Nothing, I am calling. Nothing still.

Black Rose

Your not being here —
angel in diminutive,
double negative —
would feel not fair.

Plum

Minute by minute they live:
The stone's in the midst of all.

1

We were to prune our plum.
The weather's been damp lately
and the chainsaw that we have is electric.
We went about other stuff for the time being.
First hint of warm and dry,
the plum sprung suddenly.
Its blossom is manifold, heavy,
swooping all over next door's drive.
They're cool with parking on the road,
and they've just had a baby.
The stay is temporary.
Come autumn, between us, we'll talk.

2

I booted up to type and save the above.
An automated pop-up offered me
the final pleas for mercy
of a trans woman, young
and beautiful, in rural Brazil.
The footage was days old, viral.
This was to be in praise of
plum only, blossom simply.
But often poems have,
in their happening,
a truth so not simple or pretty
it gets buried properly in gaps.
This once, let's not to do that.
I hit open. That's the truth.
I hit close before it loaded,
but ever hitting open
makes me one with
the dusty flip-flops and rocks.
I haven't slept for weeks.

3

the night he   met   reverse miraculous
where meat screams   betrayed   passed with
back to life   he   being certain
and broke   awhile and said   utterly
flesh unsubstantiate   be bread again   risen
spilt blood   more sweet than   thanks
and praise   refill all of   wine
fruit   still to   ripen on the
when supper was   blushed petal   pixilated
her voice grew   utterly   near my
take   her nights in   all of
and sweet his   threefold   and eat
this is my   nature seemed   it
limbs that had   torn muscle   transformed
will be   in his turn   act
self-repealed   moments before   forgiveness asked for
when supper was   utterly   took the
stream, the horse   tumbling cloud   minute
drank from   blood   a shadow of
gave the   stone   in the midst
said take this   drink   excess of
this is my   it will   bruise
as shred tissue   scattered over   Easter
our gravel   bonnets   gathers back into
the arms of   branches of   blossom
all of you   buds   O when
cup of the   strewn   now and
new and   pollen   in time to
so that   everlasting   will be shed
we are coming   may be   bewildered
forgiven   changed, changed   are coming to
utterly   coming to you   do this
born   in memory   to you live

A Number of Owl

The twit to whom a certain nocturnal raptor hoots
from a thicket between the hockey pitches and this
is me coming to, three-ish, in solstitial gloom.
Initially, I'm into it. After a couple of minutes?
It feels too round, too routine, too self-consciously twee,
too common-or-garden realistic to ring, well, true.

What's the plural of *owl*? I should just drop it.
When you don't answer I should just leave you sleep.
Could singular and plural be the same, as with *salmon*?
To whit you growl rhetorically, 'What is he on?'
To whit you ask, 'Does *two owl* sound correct to you?'
and slip through to the room of a daughter who's poorly.

There was an interview in the *Star*: a pair of neighbours,
each at one with nature, twit-twoo-ing across allotments.
It went on years. Then their wives met at the doctor's.
They laugh now. They share a passion for Wednesday.
So, technically, there were two 'owls' present all along.
It's just that there was never any actual owl per se.

In Memory of the Recent Past

for Rachel Genn

Think of it like this:
if antiquity is
an elevation in silhouette
on the horizon,
and what we pause on
as one might a scenic overlook at evening
is present,
then past must form
the vale that falls between
in grades of recentness.
Most recent is nearest.
Too near to see,
it recedes from us as noise.
We hear it.

We mark it pending.
Not yet sufficiently distant
to laugh about,
it won't ask forgiveness
the way history does,
nor indulge us such indifferent ease.
Its dark age is more
the traumatic quotidian
of yesterday, the day before
we shared
and wish we hadn't,
the earth beneath our feet,
what happens
while we're speaking.

The recent past says *I want us back*
in the same breath
with *This can be undone*
(but never how).
It doesn't so much end
as discontinue
ad infinitum
at successive nows.
Its news is old,
if only just.
Its fruit, that looked so pretty
on the window sill
no one touched it months,
is blown with flies.

Fly we wouldn't hurt
yet somehow did,
it haunts.
Its horrors are
of small hours.
It hurts itself.
We tell it, *We're so sorry.*
We confess,
It's your very only-just-ness
that's the killer.
It's made of stuff
we can't help making more of
with every second shed
like skins, or love.

Just there, even,
in a place we're no longer.
You smiled. I smiled too.
As if we both could hear,
amidst us, a thing
that must remain implicit
to cling to living, dearly.
At the core of every waking moment
is slippage
so granular, so infinitesimal,
to be as near inaudible
as makes no difference.
We still hear it.
The trick is not to listen.

Upon the Very Nature of Loss

I return a fraction of myself. Five-sevenths?
A healthy fraction, but a fraction nonetheless.

What of that hip flask of remaindered flab?
Word has it it's — he's — been getting along famously.

Such irony! That fats burned on river tracks
to seem svelte, lovable, should club together, be so

loved by a population of greater Ulaanbaatar's worth
of friendship circle, prove even such a hit

with beached blubber at the bar of Big Jim's
beneath the iron viaduct we never enjoyed

when he and I were joined at the gut,
politic, continent with his wisdom pearls,

my walking parable, mon brotherless semblable,
mon proverbial drawer of lidless tupperware.

And bully for him, my decommissioned underbelly,
my displaced excess anti-matter gone alien,

slumming it off some or other dispensation's radar
sans green card or social security or paperwork

of any order, my lardy doppelganger,
my collapsible table, my fabulously popular surplus-

to-requirements blockbuster nom de plume
for whom one is thrilled — naturally — to bits.

Listen. If you lie one ear to the ocean floor
you all but hear the whale of a time he's having.

Bank

for Mary

Seeds of
the dandelion
picked from
millions
like it,
blown, catch bits
of sun
and carry them
downwind
a field's
length. I want
more years
together.
I walk towards
our shadow.

Appalachian Epithalamion

Thomas Kozak and Mackenzie Connellee, Blowing Rock, NC,
29 August 2015

For plural 'youse',
Dear Tom, Dear Mac,
this verse meringue,
archaic cake
of words. Its make?
Part Jew's harp twang,
part campest tack,
part borrowed blues.

To know what note
to strike is tough.
A splash of soul
and less 'ornate'?
The altered state,
the open goal,
of mystic stuff
that hippies quote?

We're getting warm.
The time's nigh when
we slake our thirst
on *thine*s and *thou*s
betrothed espouse.
But business first:
disclaimers, then
remarks on form.

No metaphors
were hurt to hatch
this song, nor dogs,
nor muses harmed,
nor garters charmed
by dancing clogs
and Appalach-
ian dulcimers.

One line, two feet . . .
Think touching hands.
Think sump pump's click
beneath the floor.
Think seeds and core.
Think eightsome slick
rococo dance
whose middles meet.

You dig? Ye gods . . .
So 2's the room
that luck frequents.
O sing its brace
of pulses, praise
that deuce from whence
all evens bloom
against all odds.

Come harvest corn.
Or, better still,
come dial a mix
as filled the floor
in clubs of yore,
all *tweens* and *twixts*,
all froth and frill
till rosy morn.

Make light of vows.
Make music of
the flame, the moths,
the echo rings,
such hollow things,
such *hath*s and *doth*s,
as love and love
alone allows.

Make chastity
a drag, a chore,
a blinding sun.
Go pick the locks
of paradox.
You're almost one!
All truth's a door
and here's the key.

By true mean false
to sorrows past
in present tense,
the *joie de vivre*
of make-believe,
uncommon sense,
where first goes last
and silence calls.

By false mean young
enough to trust
this sovereign act
of husband/wife
is afterlife
before the fact,
its ingrained dust,
its groove and tongue.

By young mean old;
by losses, wins;
by fingers, lips;
by war and peace,
the birds and bees;
by moon, eclipse . . .
Each end begins
in summer's cold.

Its cross is hard
to bear alone.
It's time. Say yes.
This day will fall
from grace with all
the weightlessness
of pages blown
around a yard.

Today's the day
when hitters switch,
the circle squares,
the shadow doubts
its dark and clouds
en masse disperse,
that *Diem* which
one must *Carpe*.

Today's the pill
to pop, the sum
that comes of parts,
the one to seize
and make a breeze
with happy hearts
of grief and hum,
'I will, I will.'

This day's a new
that's ageless boon.
In answer to
the preacher dude's
'Do you? Do you?'
just sigh and swoon
'I do! I do!'
Then do. Then do.